BLACKBOARD BLUNDERS

Spelling Slip-ups and Homework Howlers

Richard Benson

CONTENTS

INTRODUCTION

Kids are notorious for saying the funniest things, but often their writing offers gems of equal hilarity. The riotous mistakes that can emerge when children put pen to paper in an effort to express themselves would put an experienced wordsmith to shame and bring down the house in a comedy show. Yet the beauty of these errors – especially those which turn out to be nothing short of profane – is that their perpetrators are blissfully unaware of the blunder they've just made.

Sometimes the mistake, however funny, has the makings of a truly profound statement. Take, for example, the earnest and oddly accurate assertion that, 'We have to look after the sky. Polution can spoil it and so can spraying too many arsols.' Others, however, are just plain silly. It is difficult to imagine how the following situation would come about: 'I dident get to sleep mutch because next doors dog was baking all night.'

You are sure to find plenty in this book to laugh about.

You've been warmed!

I ♥ SCHOOL

mrs Pearson said I could stay in at playtime and help her sick up some pictures on the wall.

The headteacher likes to snivel around on a black chair in his office.

My teacher said I was very epidemically bright. I was prowed!

The scool hell is being painted so we had assembily in our classroom.

If you are really naughty

you get exploded from school.

The teacher looked at Mark and growled, 'I expose you think that's clever!'

When we did the coin game I was the looker and Mark was the tosser.

We was playing futbol and we fell and we started to have a fit. It was not a bad fit but the teacher tolled us of.

Once there was a dog in the playground and we went to smoke it but the dinner lady told us to keep away.

Yesterday, Bert asked if he could burrow my football shorts at break time.

There are lots of birds in the school garden. The other day I saw some tits and a chaffage. The chaffage was pink and grey.

I ♡ SCHOOL

Teecher said I couldn't do PE because
I hadn't brot my pimps.

My favorit game at playtime is stock in
the mud and playing with the dope.
I can use a skiping dope on my own.

We wieghed the school rabbi today, it was two killer grans. When he becomes four killer grans, we haf to put him on a diet.

When PC Handley visited he had a helmet and a smart white shit.

The teacher in deception class looked across the room and shouted 'Slop that at once!' That was a surprise.

I ♡ SCHOOL

I am verry verry sorry. It is wrong
to keep giving massages to my friends
when I should be listening to the
teacher. I will not do it again.

I found a spare seal so I
quickly sat on it.

In the playground we play docters and and nurses but I got told off. I got told off because Henry had a sore throet and I put a stick on his tunge to see inside. The stick was from a tree.

I scored the winning goat in our football match, the minger was really impressed.

THE ARTS

Today I painted an octopuss with big eyes and eight purple testicles.

Lowry's pictures were mostly about the different prats of Manchester.

I'm good at sewing, I will be able to run up curtains soon.

You have to boo early for the School play.

I love drawing and painting so my favourite subject is ars.

I luv J. K. Rolling, she is my heroin.

When you write a story you should do a daft copy first. Then you can change it round and make it sound better.

If you don't want to use a full stop you can use an exsitement mark instead.

'You are under A rest and you will be remembered in custard for the night,' said the policeman. He wasn't expecting that!

In the next part of the story, the judge condomned the prisoner to death.

The pilot was bound to crash the plane. The moment he saw his wig come loose and fall to the ground he knew there was no chance of survival.

'And now' declared Mr Scarlett-Jones 'I shall read your uncles last will and testacle.'

The two cars sped down the road. The crooks had stolen the Jagger but the police were catching up fast with there top of the range Grandad.

She went mad and they put her in the menstral institution.

Robert was In a very bad crash and he has not wocken up from it.
I think he is in a cromer.

The driver flashed at me so I decided to cross the road.

there was an acident on our road last night and a man was badly enjoyed.

Time seemed to be standing still. Nothing was happening and I was getting scarred. I looked again at my cock. It hadn't moved since I last looked at it.

The whistle sounded and smoke pumed from the ship's flannel.

The magician tapped on his majik box and said 'abracadabra' and then varnished from under the table.

'Look at your hands!' said Mrs Grumble. 'I don't know where you've been but they're as black as the arce of spades!'

As he stepped outside he gave a quick nob of his head and everybody knew what he meant.

There was a very thick frog on the roads last night and it maid a car crash into a bus.

Mr. Brown walked into the room and
sat on his favourite choir.

In last year's ~~Christmas~~ Christmas concert,
Linzi played the main prat. I played
one of the smaller prats and I would
like to have a bigger prat this year.

... and at the end of the show we all sing away in a manager.

When my big sister palyed Glodilocks I was aloud in the concert too. I just had to be a little bare.

GEOGRAPHY

The north pole is so cold that the people that live there have to live sumewhere else.

You use the 24 hour clock in summer because it stays light longer.

The closet town to France is Dover. You can get to France on a train or you can go on a fairy.

In geography we learned that countries with sea round them are islands and ones without sea are incontinents.

They used to think the earth was fat but it is really round. It is shaped like a spear.

In Scandinavia, the Danish people
come from Denmark, the Norwegians
come from Norway and the
Lapdancers come from Lapland.

A flat mop of the world is an atless.
A round mop is a glob.
Globs are more intresting.

I feel sorry for children in Africa. They are staring to death. They only get a little groin to eat. I would not like to eat the groin.

We lernt about africa in geography class, I would like to see the wild breasts roaming the plans.

A ship's window is called a pothole.

There are lots of carnivorous forests in Scotland. And in the forest you can see dears and slags.

MATHS

I need to work herd on my maths so I will be god at it.

We drew a giraf to show how many trafics went passed the school.

Frackchens are like harvs quarters and tirds.

I would like to be an accountant but you have to know a lot about moths.

Two halves make a whale.

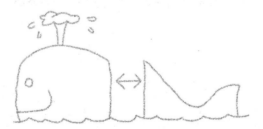

The total is when you add up all the numbers and a remainder is an animal that pulls santa on his slay.

The most popular crisps were salt and vinegar and the least popular were ready slated.

if you gess but you dont gess hiy enuf Yu undress to mate.

If it is less than 90 degrees it is a cute angel.

SCIENCE

One of the most important farces is the farce that pulls things to the ground. This farce is called gravy

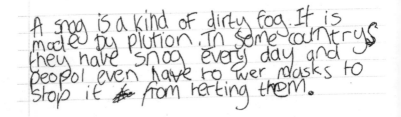

A snog is a kind of dirty fog. It is mocled by plution. In some countrys they have snog every day and peopol even have to wer masks to stop it from herting them.

Today our teecher tort us about the new Hardon Collider—when it's turned on it could corse a big bang.

YOU CAN GET AN ELECTRIC SHOCK FROM A PYTHON AND BE KILLED.

Helicopters are cleverer than planes. Not only can they fly through the air they can also hoover.

Our solar system is made of a sun, nine planets, lots of moons and balls of fire which fly around inside the system and can cause damage. These are called hemaroids.

If there are alons out in space I would like for them to come to earth and say hello. Or whatever you say if you are an alan.

We can all see things because we have a septic nerve that joins our eyes to our brians.

The sun rises in the east and sets in the west.
That is why it's hotter in the east.

Computers have made our lives
easier. But sometimes do not.
They often break down And
we get sperm-mail.

HISTORY

Sir Walter Raleigh circumcised the world with a big clipper.

my favourite subject is history. i like looking into the post to see what i can find.

If you had no money in the 1930s you could get some by going to the porn shop. The man at the porn shop had 3 balls hanging over his entrance.

Then Joan of Ark met her end. She was burned as a steak.

We buy poopies and weare them all week. On poopy day we all go quiet and think about dead people.

In the olden days cars were not aloud to go fast. The first cars had to follow a man with a fag in his hand.

For the frist time in history people could have mashines to help them with their work at home You could have a Frig in your kichen.

In wartime children who lived in big cities had to be evaporated because it was safer in the country.

If you did something brave in the war you might get a meddle.

florence

Sugar Lump

Florence nitingale was known as the lady with the lump.

In the oldern days the streets were very bumpy because they were full of Cobblers.

SOMETIMES IN THE WAR THEY TAKE PRISNERS AND KEEP THEM AS OSTRIGES UNTIL THE WAR IS OVER. SOME PRISNERS END UP IN CONSTERPATION CAMPS.

Captain Cok was a famos exploder. He soiled the seas in his soiling ship.

There are two houses of parliament in our country. The main one is the house of Comons. The other is the house of lords.

I had traveled back in time to the war, I tried to buy a drink but I only had new money on and it was going to cost me a shitting. What could I do?

In the field near our house they think they have found the remains of a Roman fart.

After the war they had to build houses quickly to replace the ones that had been bombed. These houses were called perverts. There are still some old perverts around today.

The sultanas had wifes and also porcupines

The Easter game of egg rolling started in deberhams and Cornwall.

Dico dansing started when my mum was young. Before that there was lots of other danse fashions. In the 1920s there were girls called floppers...

Greek Gods

The three gods in my project are the king of gods – Zeus, the messenger of the gods – Hermes, and the god of war – Arse.

The sufrajets complaned
for voles for women.

WHAT I DID ON MY HOLIDAYS...

On ar activity holiday Dad wanted
to ride the hores, but mom said
they were too ekspensiv.

We spend two weeks in grease every year.

My uncle Steve took my cusins to Blackpool to see the aluminashons. We went to Blackpool as well but we went to see the lights.

We nearly ran over a peasant in the weekend. It ran out from a framyard.

This holiday we got some slobs to make a patio in the back garden.

Some of the biggest fish my dad had caught are from our holidays. He has caught pikes and craps.

Wen we were in Scotland we used to go into the woods for a walk. Dad liked to see how many beers he could see.

When it gets neer Crismas I get choclat penis. I get one evry morning.

Santa carries all the toys in a big sock on his back.

Last chrismas I herd Santa putting the presents in our living room. He nocked over something and swored like daddy.

It was peek season when we went on holiday to the beach; there were ladles in bikinis everywhere.

this is a piktur of my mum sellin speydls.

RELIGIOUS STUDIES

Dear God,
My wish is that there wood be pis all
over the world. Make the wars end and
and let pipol live in pis all their lives...

The church near my hous is three
hundred years away, we go there
on wholly days and Sindays.

Jesus died cross, he had bleeding feet and he was stoned.

If you marry two people you are a pigamist, but morons are allowed to do this.

I did a cak stall for charity, i sold all my caks. The Cristian charity was a non-prophet organisation.

A mosque is a sort of church. The main difference is that its roof is doomed.

In jewish churches they do not have vickers. Insted they have rabbits.

Jesuses dad was joseøf. He was
a crapinter.

Adam was lonely so he made Eve
out of a apple tree.

The most famus of the ten commendments is thou shall comment on a duckery.

Monks are men who give their life to God and marry nuns. They live in a monstery.

I asked my mum why we said old men at the end of prayers at skool, I don't know any old men apart from grandpa.

All over the world there are different religons. The people dress different and do different things but one thing is the same. They all worship agog.

NATURAL HISTORY

Every living thing is an orgasm.
From the smallest cell to a
whole mammal, there are
orgasms everywhere.

In Australia they have small
kangaroos as well. They are called
wallies.

Baby cows are chars and baby bulls
are bollocks.

My hobby is insest. I lern about all kinds of insest from a book I bort at the bring and bye sale. I speshly like aunts.

Ostralia is famos for its speshal animals like kangeroos, cola bears and cookobuggas. You cant get this anymer els.

The best place to put pants is somewhere warm and damp, where they can live happily.

That is the end of my project on porkypines. My next one will be about armydildos.

we have to look after the sky.
poolution canspoil) it and so<an spraying
too many arsals.

I like to pik up smells on the beach
and keep them in my room.

Crap rotation is what farmers do when they have groan the same crap in a field for a long time.

Crabs and creatures like them all belong to a family of crushed asians.

The jungles of Africa are very dangerous for the people who explore them. There must be hundreds of people who have been mauled to death by a tiger or lino.

... and there are monkeys with red bottoms called buffoons.

Fax hunting is cruel. Faxes can be a bit of a newsance at times, specially if they come at night but it is still wrong to get crowds of people and dogs to rip the poor little faxes to shreds. I think fax hunting should be made iligitimate.

FOOD

Every morning dad has a slice of dread before he goes to work.

Last week it was Jack's berthday. He bront a cak to school and we all had a pis. I had a pink pis.

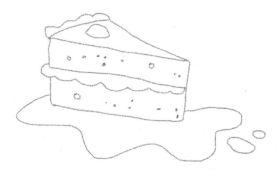

The best dinner is spagete bolonase. Its main ingredents are pasta, sause and minge meat.

All our family love sweats. I like sticky buns with icing on top but my mum is the worsed. She loves bras of chocolate. She had three chocolate bras on friday evening last week.

When we go and see my
nan she always gives
us lots of nise things
to eat. My mum has a
current bum and I have
a batenball cake.

We got our tea from the chinees
last night. I love omimental
food.

They couldn't fit us in for a meal at
the restraint because we hadn't
reversed a table.

On speshol ocashuns i am alowed coke.
My dad has wiskey. He says its
his farrit nipple.

You can make toste by putting
bread in a toster or by putting it
under a girl until it is done.

I FEEL SICK!

I went to see the docter because I keep getting orful crap. I woak up with the crap all down my leg yesterday and I cuddent put my foot down.

The densits sicked a sicker on my frunt for being gud.

If you feel portly go to the nurse or docter.

I brock my tooth and I had to get a feeling from the dentist.

Safety is very impotent. My brother was unsafe on his bikeycle and he fell off and broked a bone in his back called his cockstick.

I FEEL SICK!

I keep getting whacks in my ear and it makes me a bit def. I think the docter will try to suck it out.

I was scarred of going to the bentist but I just felt a little prick and went to sleep.

Sometimes if you are reely reely poorly you go to a speshal ward in hospital and the ward is called insensitive care.

After I saw the school nurse I felt butter, on the hole.

My brother broked his humorous bone in his arm, he had a plaster put on and a large slong.

HOME TIME

I hepled my dad in the garage. He let me hit some nails in with his hamster.

for my praty we went to the blowing alley. When we had been blowing we had a drink and a buger.

At brownies this week we ~~been~~ lernt to do sin language. I lernt fensing too. Fensing is when you fight with a sod.

...and then Mr. Browning showed us how climbers use tampons to grip on to their roc.

... and tow times a week we have a nashonal lottery. There are six balls and a boxeless ball.

I go to St Johns to lern fisk aid. I have lernt how to do a bondage and I got to practice on Mr Terry. He is the leader.

I take the dog for a walk in the park every morning.

The girl who collects our rent has stopped coming. Now we have a rent boy instead.

My tummy rambles after school so I have choclet suggestives when I get home.

I saw some grillers at the zoo,
they werr big and herry Like my dad.

My mum falled down the stairs and
was lying prostitute on the ground.

My mum saw my messy bedroom and said it was abdominal. I felt a lot of quilt.

Dad talked about weapons of mass digestion while eating dinner. I'm worried about this — I don't want to get bumbed.

My dad luvs watching the footy — he says it's poultry in motion.

I used to not like our pet dog because he was viscose, he has groaned on me now.

My mum keeps ghosts in our garden,
they keep nippling the washing.

We had a swimming pull dug in our
garden and my dad filled it with
his big nose.

FRIENDS AND FAMILY

my grandad has got a huge organ. he says one day he will give it to me but I have to lern how to play it.

This wikend we went shoping. I got some new shoes and mummy got a new pair of tits.

when I was foul, I had a speshul party and a cak which I shaved with all my firends.

Mum and dad were panting in my bedroom this weekend. They panted it blue and stuck a cute boarder round the middle.

Mummy had been in the bath and when she dryed her her hair she saw her bush was missing. We all lookd for it but daddy let her have his coom.

I have lots of fiends at school and I have even more fiends at home.

and I took a bunch of violents home for my mum.

We have found out that anty Mary is stagnant and she will be having a baby in March.

The funny thing about my family is that they are all divers. My uncle Tim is a taxi diver, my uncle Steve is a bus diver and my Dad is a van diver.

My mum goes to jim every freday.
She always comes home too tired to do
anything.

We went to visit my dad's boss this holiday.
He lives in a big hose.

Every time we go shopping we have the same fuss. Dad wants to read the Mirror and mum wants her Daily Male.

We took my baby sister to the panto for the frist time this year. We went to see Seeping Beauty.

We are taking my little sister to see
Satan this weekend.

On Sunday my dad filmed me falling into
our pond by axident. We are going to
send it to You've Been Farmed.

My mum writes the chek out and my dad looks at it and sins.

My dad looks silly. He has groan a bread. He had a must dash befor but I thinck his bread looks silly.

My grandad yoused to be a cool miner wen he was young.

My uncle had to wipe the widows with a wet cloth yestday because the rain made them derty.

Dad was working in the garden and he ▰
ascked mum if she could come and give
him a hard. She was bisy so aunty jo
went instead.

My mum was a bit Shook up yesterday
because she had a dump in the car.

Since her axident my mum has to go to a fizzy therapist every week.

My uncle is impotent.

He is the boss of a big factory.

Mummy givs chang for the slat mashins and baddy is a dingo Calver.

My gran has a huge chest. We keep our toys in it.

My unck jake died last week and he still isent better.

Grandad aont let me have his old programmes because he wants to keep keep them for his pasterior.

My dad took me dog racing on Sunday, my favrit was a cocky spaniard,

WHEN I
GROW UP

I like sewing. I would like to
be a sewer when I grow up. I am
helping my mum make a
pachwork kilt.

when I grow up I want to learn
how to tipe quickly and I want
to be a tipissed.

I would like to be a Signtist and I would
like to work in a lavatory.

My uncle shouts at my cussins and makes them do chors. One day they are going to be polisemen and polisewomen so they can put him in prison.

I wuld like to be a vet becouse I enjoy mreating animals.

My sister is a babyseller. She gets money from the grown ups, and sells their babys while they are away. I would like to be a babyseller too.

WHEN I AM OLDER I WANT TO LEARN TO DRIVE A CAT.

I would love to have lots of babys when I'm a grownup. My mummy says I have to wait untill I'm much older but tina across our road has lots of babys and she isnt grownup. She also has lots of husbends.

I am going to be a scientologist because I am cleaver at science.

611

My dad wants me to be a
nurse but I want to be a dancer. But
I can do both. Work in the day
time and a dancer in the night time.
He says this could be true because he
once knew of ladys who did that.

BEDTIME

My sister is 3. When she goes to bed she calls
her blanket a wanket. It makes my mum and
big sister larf.

I dident get to sleep mutch because
next doors dog was baking all night.

My little sister still has to sleep with the
light on because she is afraid of the dork.

Befor i go to bed i sometimes hav a mug ful of
warmed up milk to help me go to sleep. Mummy has
mug ful of wine.

My dad works nights so he spends all
day in deb.

BEDTIME

My baby bother Sleeps in a cat in my bedroom.

It is verry noisy at night for me because we live above a pube.

... and suddenly the door opened and banged against the wall. I felt a lamp in my throte.

I sleep in my bedrom. My broter sleeps in his bedrom. My mummy sleeps in hers and daddys bedrom but daddy sumtimes sleeps on the sofa with our dog. I think this is because he grawls like a dog when he is snooring in his sleep.

Sam's mum looked at her little boy. 'Come on, it's up to the land of nod for you.' she said.

F IN EXAMS
The Best Test Paper Blunders

Richard Benson

ISBN: 978 1 84024 700 8   Paperback   £5.99

We've all been there. You've been studying hard, the day of the BIG test arrives, you turn over the paper, and 'what the *&%@ does that mean?!' Not a clue.

This book is packed full of hilarious examples of the more creative ways that students have tackled those particularly awkward exam questions.

'Some great examples of exam answers from the most clueless – and inventive – of students'   timesonline.co.uk

Have you enjoyed this book?
If so, why not write a review
on your favourite website?

Thanks very much for buying
this Summersdale book.

www.summersdale.com